NATIONAL GEOGRAPHIC

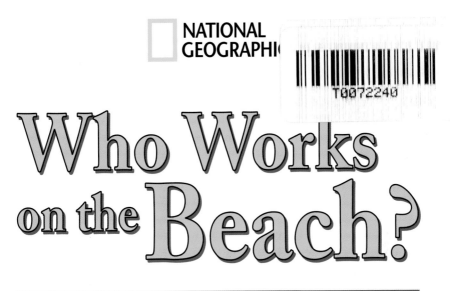

Who Works on the Beach?

Claude Wright

I work on the beach.

I sell ice cream and drinks.

I help people cool off.

3

I work on the beach.

I pick up trash left on the sand.

I help keep the beach clean and safe.

5

I work on the beach.

I watch the swimmers.

I help people stay safe in the water.

I work on the beach.

I rent sailboats.

I help people sail on the sea.

9

I work on the beach.

I teach people how to windsurf.

I help people have fun in the water.

Many people work on the beach.
They make it a fun place to visit.